SHARKS

Wildlife Monographs – Sharks
Copyright ©2005 Evans Mitchell Books

Text and Photography Copyright ©2005 Jonathan Bird

First published in the United Kingdom by:
Evans Mitchell Books
Norfolk Court, 1 Norfolk Road,
Rickmansworth, Hertfordshire WD3 1LA
United Kingdom

Jacket and Book Design by:
Roy Platten
Eclipse
roy.eclipse@btopenworld.com

British Library Cataloguing in Publication Data.
A CIP record of this book is available on request
from the British Library.

ISBN: 1-901268-11-X

10 9 8 7 6 5 4 3 2 1

Pre Press: F.E Burman, London, United Kingdom

Printed in Thailand

SHARKS

JONATHAN BIRD

Evans Mitchell Books

Contents

Introduction

Since the release of the film, *Jaws,* the shark has suffered from an unfair and grossly exaggerated reputation. Reviled or feared as maneaters, sharks have been relegated to the category of monster in many people's minds. In fact, this couldn't be further from the truth. Sharks are highly evolved animals just trying to survive. They are no more dangerous to people than any large predator, like a lion or a bear, and statistically pose almost no threat to people.

Sharks have amazing senses that biologists do not fully understand, and powerful immune systems that might teach humankind how to defeat many diseases. We stand to learn much from sharks, and they deserve our respect and admiration. Sharks have an important role in ocean ecosystems at the top of the food chain. Without them to prey upon the sick and weak, other animals in the ocean might overgrow their food resources and even lose their evolutionary impetus.

Above: Perhaps no sight is as terrifying as a fin slicing through the water – shark! This metre high fin belongs to the harmless Basking shark *(Cetorhinus maximus)*, but it closely resembles the fin of a Great white. Often the harmless Basking shark is mistaken for a monstrous Great white.

Opposite: The streamlined proportions of the Caribbean Reef shark *(Carcharhinus perezi)* are what most people think of when you mention a shark.

Very few cultures actually eat sharks, yet ironically, sharks are being killed at record levels, both for their fins and when they are accidentally caught in trawler nets. With their low reproductive rate and long gestation period, sharks are among the slowest fishes to reproduce, making them highly susceptible to overfishing.

Wildlife Monographs – Sharks provides a fascinating look into the lives of sharks in the hope that readers might be motivated towards becoming a part of the growing movement to protect the endangered shark populations around the world.

Below: The Caribbean Reef shark *(Carcharhinus perezi)* doesn't look very toothy at first glance. It's teeth are hidden when its mouth is closed. But this shark has an impressive set of teeth that can take huge bites out of its prey. This robust shark reaches 3 metres.

Opposite: Reaching up to 15 metres in length and 12,000 kg, the Whale shark *(Rhincodon typus)* is the largest fish in the world, yet it is completely harmless to people. It feeds on plankton and schools of small fishes.

Natural History

Sharks and their direct predecessors have been swimming in the world's oceans for well over 350 million years. Primordial sharks hunted the seas 100 million years before dinosaurs walked the Earth. In fact, before animals even existed on land, sharks swam in the oceans. These early sharks resembled their modern descendants, but had a long way to go before they would be as evolved and refined as modern sharks.

The earliest sharks flourished and became extinct before the continents of the world began to break up and drift. Nobody knows exactly why, but the early sharks were tough and they survived mass extinctions that wiped out many of the earlier forms of bony fishes.

Above: The Great White shark *(Carcharodon carcharias)* may be the most famous shark of all time. Honed by millions of years of evolution and highly adapted to its role, the Great White is the ultimate predator of the oceans. But it's a far cry from the villain it portrayed in Jaws.

Opposite: Many sharks have countershading, a kind of camouflage where the belly is light in colour and the dorsal surface is dark. This helps the shark blend in to the bottom when viewed from above and blend into the surface when view from below. Countershading helps the Caribbean Reef shark *(Carcharhinus perezi)* sneak up on its prey.

Evolution played its vital part and the basic shark we know today emerged about 250 million years ago. In the Jurassic period, which began about 200 million years ago, dinosaurs ruled both the land and the seas. Sharks existed, but they were not the fearsome animals that the dinosaurs were. They were in fact quite small although they had most of the characteristics of modern sharks. When the mass extinction of the dinosaurs occurred however, the sharks survived.

With the seas free of ichthyosaurs and other great reptilian predators, sharks thrived. By the time the Cretaceous period rolled around, about 150 million years ago, most of the modern species we know today had become established and evolution has certainly allowed the shark to hone its senses and fit into every niche the ocean can provide.

Above: Sharks have rough, sandpapery skin. This skin, seen here on a Nurse shark (*Ginglymostoma cirratum*), is made up of thousands of tiny tooth-like structures called dermal denticles. The dermal denticles and the teeth are the only two parts of a shark that usually produce fossils, so our knowledge of ancestral sharks is very limited.

Opposite top: The fossilised tooth of a Megalodon shark (*Carcharodon magalodon*) gives an idea how big its mouth might have been. Although the teeth reached 17 cm in length, we have no idea how large this prehistoric shark might have been. Some speculate it could have eaten a fully grown horse in one bite!

Unfortunately, the cartilaginous skeleton of the shark does not form fossils well, since the soft cartilage doesn't last long enough to fossilise in most cases. So our knowledge of ancient sharks is often limited to information gained from teeth and scales, called dermal denticles, the only parts of a shark's body hard enough to readily leave a fossil.

About 50 million years ago, *Carcharodon megalodon* appeared on the scene. Certainly this must be one of the most fearsome and famous sharks of all time. The enormous 17 centimetre long fossilised teeth left behind by C. *megalodon* has left scientists wondering how big such a shark would have been. Since no skeleton has been found, it's hard to guess how big this shark actually was. Recent estimates place it in the 15 metre range, enormous for a carnivorous shark by today's standards, with a mouth large enough to eat a fully grown horse in one bite. The fossil record indicates that this shark existed up until 15 million years ago, fairly recent in geological time. Many believe that the Great white shark, *Carcharodon carcharias* is a direct ancestor of *megalodon*.

While sharks continue to evolve like all animals, the fact that they have survived for so long demonstrates the incredible effectiveness of their anatomy. It's likely that sharks will still swim in the oceans millions of years from now when humans no longer exist.

Above: Sharks have evolved amazing senses. The nasal openings on a Gray Reef shark *(Carcharhinus amblyrhynchos)* are seen in this shot. Some sharks can smell as little as a drop of blood in a million gallons of water.

Anatomy and Senses

For all their fearsome reputation, sharks are just sophisticated fish. A fish is defined as a vertebrate (an animal with a backbone) that has fins and swims. All fishes are broken into two classes. Fish such as cod or trout are members of the "bony fish" class, (called *Osteichthyes*) and are characterised by a skeleton made of bone, like humans, and a single pair of gill openings. Most also have something called a swim bladder, a balloon-like internal organ used to modulate buoyancy by adding and removing gas. A fish uses it to hover in place so it neither sinks nor floats.

Sharks occupy the other class, called *Chondrichthyes* (meaning "cartilage-fish"). Sharks and their close relatives (rays, skates, and ratfishes) differ from the bony fishes in several important ways. Among the more important, sharks have flexible cartilaginous skeletons that lack hard bone and five, six or seven gill slits on each side of their head,

Above: At a dive site known as Stingray City in the Cayman Islands, divers can hand feed Southern Stingrays *(Dasyatis Americana)*. Although these animals usually hunt for clams and worms in the sand, they have been acclimated to people by handouts. Although they have a powerful stinger at the base of their tail, Southern Stingrays are not aggressive at all.

Opposite: The Lesser Electric Ray *(Narcine brasiliensis)* can produce 35 volts to stun its prey (mostly small fishes and invertebrates). It's no threat to a diver, but its ability to generate electricity makes it fairly rare among sharks and rays.

depending on species. They also lack swim bladders. This class of fishes contains over 700 species worldwide, including over 375 species of sharks. Sharks come in many shapes and sizes. The largest fish in the ocean is, in fact, the tremendous Whale shark, reaching about 15 metres (50 feet) in length. The smallest known shark grows to only 25 centimetres (ten inches) long at full size.

Previous page: This Caribbean Reef shark *(Carcharhinus perezi)* is accompanied by a school of juvenile Bar Jacks. These fish swim with the shark for protection from larger fish. They rely on being small and manoeuverable to keep from being eaten by the shark. When the fish get older, they will no longer use the shark for protection.

Opposite top: It's hard to mistake a Whale shark *(Rhincodon typus)* – the polka-dotted pattern is unique to this shark. It probably helps the shark blend in with the light-dappled surface of the water helping it approach schools of fish to eat.

Opposite bottom: Some sharks, such as these Silky sharks *(Carcharhinus falciformis)*, can be put into a kind of hypnotic state called tonic immobility by turning them upside down and holding their tail just right. Here a diver demonstrates with two Silkies. Nobody is quite sure why this happens.

The cartilaginous skeleton makes a shark more flexible than similarly-sized bony fishes. Unfortunately, it also makes the shark a poor fossil-former, since the soft cartilaginous skeleton doesn't last long enough to fossilise in most cases. So our knowledge of ancient sharks is limited mostly to information gained from their teeth, the only part of their body that can readily leave a fossil. Since the cartilaginous skeleton is an ancient skeletal design that sharks have been using for hundreds of millions of years, many people incorrectly assume that the shark is therefore primitive. This couldn't be further from the truth.

Top: At up to 12 metres long, the Basking shark *(Cetorhinus maximus)* is the second largest fish on Earth (right behind the Whale shark). It can reach 4,500 kg but survives on nothing but planktonic crustaceans called copepods. Smaller than a grain of rice, it would take 200,000 copepods to fill a coffee cup but the massive Basking shark survives on just a copepod diet.

Bottom: A diver is dwarfed by a Whale shark *(Rhincodon typus)* in the Galapagos. It's easy to see why the shark is often compared to a whale. This shark's teeth are tiny, and completely harmless to people.

Like all fishes, sharks are heavier than water. Without something to keep them up in the water column, they sink. The shark's lack of a swim bladder means that, unlike bony fishes, the shark can't make itself neutrally buoyant, and it can't hover. A lot of sharks have a large, oil-rich liver that provides some buoyancy (oil floats on water). For example, the world's second largest fish is the Basking shark *(Cetorhinus maximus)*. Almost a third of its body weight is nothing

Opposite page: The author's wife Christine is swimming with a small Whale shark *(Rhincodon typus)*. Although some divers like to ride them, Whale sharks do not like to be touched or ridden. Even though the animal is quite large, it can feel the smallest touch against its thick skin.

Above: The remote and rough waters around Darwin Island in the Galapagos are home to massive schools of Scalloped Hammerhead sharks *(Sphyrna lewini)*. These large schools become harder and harder to see every year as the shark populations are fished. Even though sharks are protected in the Galapagos, poaching is common and hard to stop.

but its liver. A 4,000 kilogram shark may have a liver that weighs over 1,000 kilograms. But although a big liver certainly helps, it still won't make a shark neutrally buoyant. To stay off the bottom, sharks have to keep moving. While the shark uses its tail fin in a back and forth motion to provide forward thrust, its pectoral fins work like airplane wings to provide lift. Like an airplane wing, as long as the fins move forward through the water, they provide lift to keep the shark up. This lack of a swim bladder is not necessarily a weakness.

Bony fishes cannot ascend too quickly because the expanding gas in the swim bladder would cause it to rupture. They can only come to the ascend as fast as they can remove the gas from the swim bladder. The absence of a swim bladder means sharks can swim straight up as fast as they like without any danger of hurting themselves.

Right: Two Caribbean Reef sharks *(Carcharhinus perezi)* are fighting over a large piece of bait. Although this fish was completely frozen, the sharks ate it in only a few bites, their shark teeth cutting right through the rock-hard frozen fish.

Sharks are a diverse group of fish with many specialisations to survive. They inhabit all of the world's oceans, from the arctic to the tropics, from the surface to the deep-sea, and from the shoreline to the open ocean. Sharks that live in the open ocean (called pelagic sharks) can never stop to rest because they would sink thousands of feet down into the depths of the abyss, where they cannot survive due to cold water and lack of food. Such sharks usually have very large pectoral fins to act as massive wings, giving greater lift and allowing them to swim more slowly without sinking. This allows them to conserve energy and glide further with less effort.

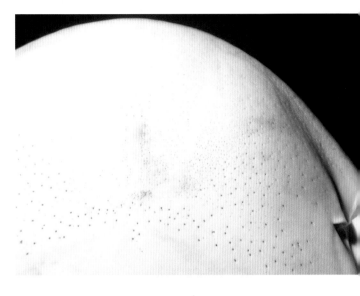

Above: Sharks have a special sense for detecting electrical currents so they can find prey using the bio-electric impulses made by the muscles of their prey. The pores on the underside of a Gray Reef shark's snout, called the ampullae of lorenzini, are the sensors of this system.

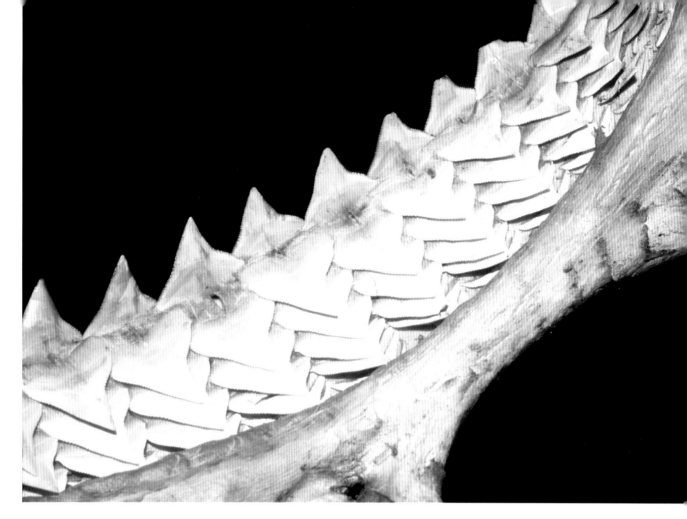

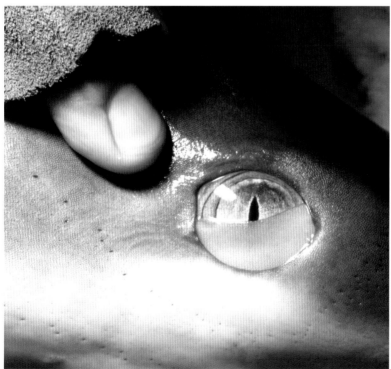

Opposite page, bottom: Nobody knows for sure why the hammerhead has its characteristic hammer-like head. Theories suggest that it may allow the shark better directional smell, better vision, more lift or even a weapon for attaching skates and rays.

Above: A Bull shark jaw. Like most sharks, Bull sharks *(Carcharhinus leucas)* have rows of developing teeth behind the active teeth. As teeth get dull or fall out, a new one rotates into place. You can count five rows of teeth waiting behind the active row in this shot.

Left: Sharks are the only fish with eyelids, called nictitating membranes, and not all shark have them. They use these eyelids to protect their eyes when attacking prey.

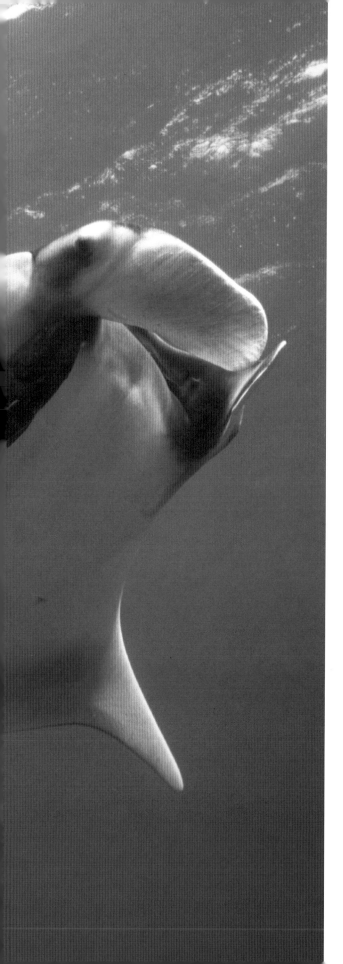

Some sharks have to keep moving so water will flow through their gills. They lack the ability to ventilate their gills when they stop. Species like the Scalloped Hammerhead *(Spherna lewini)* fall into this category. If they get caught in a net, they asphyxiate quickly. Not all sharks have to keep swimming though. Many can stop swimming and rest on the bottom, gulping water to ventilate their gills. Bottom-dwelling species of sharks like the Nurse shark *(Ginglystoma cirratus)* and Wobbegong actually live their entire lives on or near the bottom. Most species of skates and rays spend at least part of their time on the bottom.

Left: The world's largest ray is the Manta ray *(Manta birostris)* which can reach 20 feet across. This ray used to be called the Devil ray because of its cephalic fins that look like horns. Sailors thought it was a dangerous sea monster! In reality, the ray uses the cephalic fins to help scoop up tiny animals in the water called plankton. Manta rays are completely harmless to people.

Above: The teeth of the Mako shark *(Isurus oxyrinchus)* are thin and pointy, and they point backwards into the shark's mouth like the barb on a fish hook. This helps the Mako grab fish and keep them from getting away, but the teeth are not good for taking bites out of larger prey.

With such a long evolutionary history, sharks have had plenty of time to refine themselves. Recent studies have shown sharks to be remarkably sophisticated. For example, most sharks have an incredible sense of smell. Extrapolations of experiments on shark smell claim that some sharks can detect one drop of blood dissolved in as much as one million gallons of water. Such a keenly developed sense of smell leaves no doubt that a shark has few rivals in the nose department.

Sharks also have senses we can't even begin to experience. They have an electrosensory system that allows them to detect the extremely minute bio-electrical currents generated, for example, by the muscles of a swimming fish. The snout of a shark is covered in tiny pores called *Ampullae of Lorenzini,* filled with a jelly-like substance leading to nerve cells.

The *Ampullae of Lorenzini* convert electrical currents in the water to an electrical signal in the shark's nerves so that shark can sense extremely tiny electrical currents in the water. To put the sensitivity of this electro-sensory system in perspective, imagine connecting wires to a nine volt transistor radio battery and separating the ends of the wires by a kilometre. Some sharks can detect that electrical current. At close range, a fish hiding in a hole is betrayed by the electrical signature of its own heart beating.

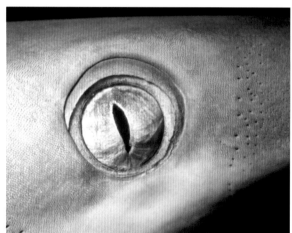

Top: A diver holding a Silky shark *(Carcharhinus falciformis)* upside down in the tonic immobility position. When he flips the shark back over and lets it go, it will swim away as if nothing happened.

Bottom: Like most sharks, the Gray Reef shark *(Carcharhinus amblyrhynchos)* has excellent eyesight, even in low light conditions, because it has a special mirror located behind the retina to reflect light through the retina twice.

Sharks can sense the tiny pressure variations generated by an injured fish struggling to swim. They do this with a system common to many fish called a lateral line. Along the sides of a shark, a series of pores contain small capsules, each containing a tiny hair-like fibre. Very small changes in water pressure cause the fibres to move, sending a signal to the shark's brain. The shark learns to recognise the "feel" of different kinds of pressure variations, such as those caused by a struggling injured fish. The shark then knows possible prey is nearby and begins to search for the fish.

Above: The shark "feeding frenzy" is a behaviour almost unknown in the wild. When a large amount of food is introduced in the vicinity of a large number of sharks, they may compete violently for food until it is all consumed. However, this rarely happens naturally. Here a large frozen fish was brought down for a group of Caribbean Reef sharks.

There is an erroneous belief that sharks have poor eyesight, but in fact most sharks have excellent eyesight, and many have simply incredible low light vision. A shiny "mirror" called the *tapetum lucidum* located behind the retina reflects light back through the retina a second time, increasing its sensitivity. At night, the eyes of these sharks reflect light the same way the eyes of cats do. Cats and sharks share similar low light adaptations of eyesight. Many sharks like to hunt at dawn and dusk, because they can see their prey much better than the prey can see them. In addition, most sharks have both rods and cones in their eyes, suggesting that they see in colour.

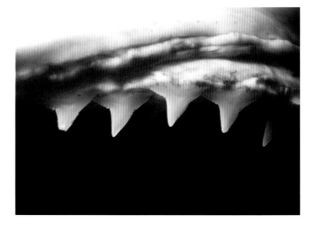

Top: Blue sharks *(Prionace glauca)* are long, skinny, and quite graceful. They are pelagic, meaning that they live far from land in the open ocean.

Bottom: The teeth of the Gray Reef shark *(Carcharhinus amblyrhynchos)* are triangular, serrated and arranged in a neat row. Designed for cutting, these teeth allow the Gray Reef shark to take a big bite out of larger prey.

Sharks never need to go to a dentist either. It's not that their teeth are any more resistant to decay or damage than any other animals, but they have many rows of disposable teeth. As old teeth break or become too dull, they fall out and new ones rotate into place from behind them. For the entire life of a shark, it never runs out of new teeth. In addition to teeth in its mouth, a shark also has a kind of "teeth" on its skin, called *dermal denticles*. These denticles, like the scales on a bony fish, all point to towards the tail. Water flows smoothly over them as the shark swims. A hand brushed from head to tail over the skin of the shark will detect a reasonably smooth surface.

Top: Scalloped Hammerheads *(Sphyrna lewini)* seem to prefer water within the narrow temperature range of 24°-26.6° C. If it's too cold or too warm, they move on to find water that is more agreeable.

Bottom: Although people used to think that all sharks had to swim to keep water moving through their gills, more and more sharks are known to rest on the bottom and pump water through their gills by "gulping." The Nurse shark *(Ginglymostoma cirratum)* is one such shark. This shark likes to feed on conchs by using a very powerful suction action to literally "inhale" them out of their shells.

31

But brush a hand backwards from tail to the head and the skin feels very rough, like sandpaper. The dermal denticles make the skin of a shark incredibly tough. In fact, some fish will sneak up and rub themselves against a shark because the sandpapery texture helps dislodge parasites.

Sharks smell better than us, hear better than us, see better than us in low light, recognise electrical signals to which we are completely blind and have a never-ending supply of teeth. Do they sound primitive? Certainly not!

The more we learn about sharks, the more we discover how little we know about them. Far from being the horrific monsters we have been lead to believe they are, sharks are actually highly evolved and sophisticated animals with a range of senses and abilities unmatched in the animal world. The study of sharks may teach us many things about our world and maybe even about ourselves.

Above: The Tasseled Wobbegong shark (*Eucrossorhinus dasypogon*) looks very different from what most people imagine in a shark. It lives camouflaged on the bottom, blending silently into the sea floor and patiently waiting for unwary fish to swim by. Then, it lunges and gulps down its unsuspecting prey.

Opposite: A Whale shark (*Rhincodon typus*) barely moves its tail when it swims, but people can only keep pace for a minute or two.

Habitat and Diet

Sharks live in every saltwater environment on Earth, and even a few freshwater environments as well. They are found from the shallows to the depths, near shore to the open ocean, and from the arctic to the tropics.

Many species of sharks like the Megamouth shark (*Megachasma pelagios*) and Goblin shark (*Mitsukurina owstoni*) live in the depths of the ocean, rarely seen alive by humans. The Great white (*Carcharodon carcharias*) prefers shallow, coastal areas in cooler temperate waters (water that is warmer than the arctic but cooler than the tropics). The Tiger shark (*Galeocerdo cuvier*) likes coastal tropical areas. The Greenland shark (*Somniosus microcephalus*) lives in the icy waters of the arctic and Bull sharks (*Carcharhinus leucas*) although they are usually found in shallow tropical seas, can make their way hundreds of miles up freshwater rivers looking for food. They have even been caught in a few lakes! With around 375 species of sharks swimming through the world's oceans, it's not surprising that they have adapted to live everywhere.

Above: This Galapagos Sea Lion (*Zalophus californianus wollebaeki*) has been bitten by a shark and survived. Many sea lions are not so lucky. They are a favourite meal of Great White sharks.

Opposite: A Caribbean Reef shark (*Carcharhinus perezi*) patrolling a wreck in the Bahamas. While many people worry about being attacked by sharks, the fact is that without chum in the water, most divers will never even see a shark. Scuba bubbles tend to frighten sharks and only bait will bring them close enough for pictures.

Pelagic sharks like the Blue shark *(Prionace glauca)* and Oceanic White tip shark *(Carcharhinus longimanus)* live in the open ocean, far from land. They almost never frequent the shallows close to shore. Because food is scarce in the open ocean, they wander hundreds, sometimes thousands of miles looking for food. The Blue shark has one of the longest known migrations in the animal world, travelling from the western Atlantic in the spring and summer, to the eastern Atlantic in the fall and winter. This migration is believed to be part of the reproductive cycle because the sharks seem to have particular areas where they like to mate and give birth. Pelagic sharks have extra long pectoral fins to provide a lot of lift at low speed, for gliding long distances with minimal effort.

Opposite left: Scalloped Hammerheads *(Sphyrna lewini)* often school around the shallows in order to be cleaned by smaller fishes. Here a crew of King Angelfish *(Holacanthus passer)* clean a hammerhead that is hovering in the current. Cleaning helps the sharks get rid of parasites and provides a meal for the cleaner fishes.

Left: After it has accumulated plenty of food on its gill rakers, the Basking shark *(Cetorhinus maximus)* closes its mouth and swallows.

Above: The Basking shark *(Cetorhinus maximus)* has a cavernous mouth several feet across, but it's harmless to people because it only eats tiny planktonic animals. Its throat is only large enough to swallow a grapefruit!

Many other sharks hardly move more than a few hundred yards in a year. Sharks like the Tasselled Wobbegong shark *(Eucrossorhinus dasypogon)* or Horn shark *(Heterodontus francisci)* live on the bottom all the time. They have the ability to ventilate their gills without swimming, and find everything they need around shallow reefs on the bottom, rarely straying far from a small home range.

Top and right: The Basking shark *(Cetorhinus maximus)* is like a big swimming strainer. It opens its mouth wide and swims through the water, scooping up the plankton. The water and plankton go into the mouth, but the water comes back out through the gill slits, while the plankton gets stuck on comb-like strainers in the gills called gill rakers.

Opposite: From behind, the massive gill slits of the Basking shark *(Cetorhinus maximus)* can be seen. They are so large that they go almost all the way around the animal's body.

Sharks eat a wide variety of foods, and in fact most prefer fairly small prey. Blue sharks eat small fishes and cephalopods (mostly squid). Hammerheads prefer squid. Even the mighty Great white shark, known for its love of marine mammals like sea lions and seals, sometimes eats fish and invertebrates like lobster and crabs when it gets the chance. Most sharks are opportunistic when it comes to food. They will eat whatever they can catch and swallow. But their ability to catch and eat certain prey is a function of their design. For example, the Sand Tiger shark *(Carcharias taurus)* has very skinny, pointy teeth that are great for grabbing small fishes and swallowing them whole, but not very good for taking bites out of larger prey. So even though the Sand Tiger is a pretty big shark, over 3 metres long, it never eats large prey, but only catches small fishes.

Similarly, the Whale shark *(Rhincodon typus)* which happens to be not just the largest shark in the world, but the largest fish as well (up to 15 metres), eats very small fishes and even plankton, which it gulps from the water in enormous mouthfuls, and strains from the water using filters in its gills. The Basking shark *(Cetorhinus maximus)* is the second largest fish in the world, reaching 12 metres. It swims through the water with its enormous mouth open to allow planktonic crustaceans called copepods to collect on its branchial sieves. These are comb-like filters on its gills that allow water to pass through but catch the plankton.

Every once in a while the shark stops swimming and swallows the collected plankton. Here is an animal that weighs 4,000 kilograms, feeding on animals smaller than a grain of rice. It takes millions and millions of copepods every day to feed a hungry Basking shark.

Many sharks in fact do prey on large animals. The Great white prefers marine mammals like seals and sea lions. It attacks them from below, striking quickly from the shadowy depths, and taking one big bite.

Right: One of the most recognisable sharks in the sea, the Great White *(Carcharodon carcharias)* shark can grow to 6.3 metres and 2,300 kg. This shark prefers to eat large mammals like seals and sea lions. Once it feeds on a sea lion, it might not eat again for weeks.

Left: From the front, the long pectoral fins of the Oceanic White tip shark *(Carcharhinus longimanus)* are obvious. Because this shark is pelagic, living in the open ocean, it needs long pectoral fins to provide lift so it can cruise slowly, conserving energy, and not sink.

Below: Also pelagic, the Blue shark *(Prionace glauca)* gets its name from its velvety blue dorsal side. This Blue shark was photographed in the north Atlantic off the east coast of the United States.

Opposite top: Blue sharks *(Prionace glauca)* often closely approach camera gear to investigate. The camera and strobes produce tiny electrical signals that the sharks can detect with their electrosensory system. They investigate to see if it might be food. Curiously, the sharks are typically quite gentle.

Opposite bottom: Not your typical shark, the Tasselled Wobbegong shark *(Eucrossorhinus dasypogon)* lives on the bottom, camouflaged. It might not move more than a few feet in a day as it waits for unsuspecting prey to come too close. The fleshy tabs hanging off its body are part of the disguise.

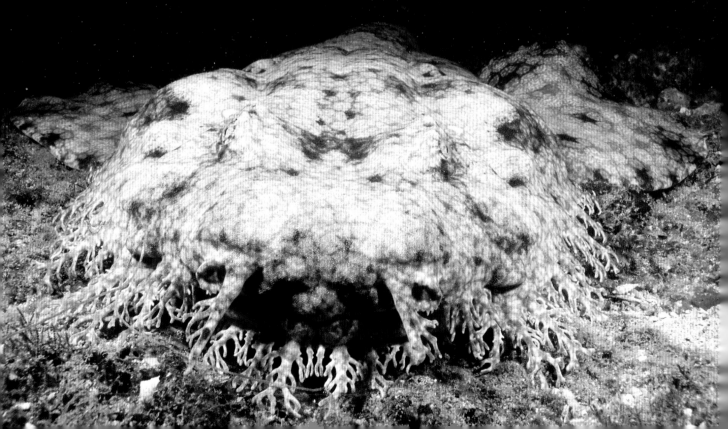

Then it waits while the seal bleeds to death. Once the animal is dead, it won't fight back, and the shark can take its time feeding. This is the reason why surfers are sometimes the victims of Great white attacks, and also the reason why most of these surfers survive.

A person paddling a surfboard looks a lot like a sea lion from below. It's likely a case of mistaken identity. The shark sees a familiar looking shape, and strikes quickly. But then it bites a surfboard, which doesn't seem right. It circles to see what happened, realises that it didn't bite a sea lion, and moves on. Sometimes these attacks are fatal, but most of the time, the victim survives.

Tiger sharks also like large prey. They seem to prefer sea turtles, and have a very sharp set of teeth designed like a saw blade for cutting through the tough shell of a sea turtle. But in a pinch, a Tiger shark will eat all kinds of fishes – even other sharks.

Top: When Scalloped hammerheads *(Sphyrna lewini)* come to a "cleaning station" to be cleaned by King Angelfish, they have to swim really slowly because the Angelfish won't stray far from their "turf." If the current is strong enough, a hammerhead can swim in place, as if on a treadmill. That allows it to hover right over the cleaning station and many fish will often come to clean the shark.

Right: Sand Tiger sharks *(Carcharias Taurus)* have a mouthful of impressive teeth. The long, pointy teeth are designed to grab and hold small fishes so they can't get away. This coupled with the fact that they are easy to keep alive in captivity makes them popular in large public aquaria.

Opposite bottom: Great White shark *(Carcharodon carcharias)*.

Left: Blue sharks *(Prionace glauca)* make one of the longest migrations in the animal world. In the Atlantic, they migrate between the coast of the United States in the summer to the coast of Europe in the winter. Tagging studies have proved that the sharks might migrate as much as 8,000 km a year!

Below: A group of Nurse sharks *(Ginglymostoma cirratum)* are resting on the bottom during the day, because they are mostly active at night, using the darkness to their hunting advantage.

Opposite top: This Oceanic White tip shark *(Carcharhinus longimanus)* has a fisherman's hook stuck in its mouth. It was a lucky shark that got away. Sharks are under tremendous pressure from overfishing and shark populations are dwindling all over the world.

Opposite bottom: This Southern Stingray *(Dasyatis Americana)*, a close relative of sharks, is feeding in the sand. Like a swimming metal detector, it finds worms and clams in the sand using it's keen electrosensory system, then slurps them up. It's mouth is underneath its body.

The amazing adaptability of sharks means that they have colonised the entire ocean, and eat just about anything available. With so many different kinds of sharks occupying so many different places in the food web, it's understandable that sharks would have a wide variety of foods upon which they feed. More than 95% of the sharks in the oceans pose absolutely zero threat to people. Of the small percentage that might do, humans are not the food of choice, so the chances are pretty good that none of us will ever end up on the menu.

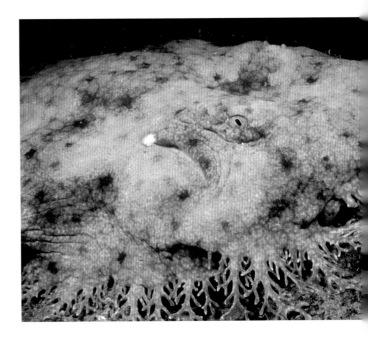

Above: Sharks live in every marine habitat on Earth from the surface to the deep sea and from shallow coastal waters to the open ocean far from land. Sharks like the Wobbegong prove that not all sharks look alike.

Left: The Mako shark *(Isurus oxyrinchus)* is one of a few species that is semi-warm-blooded. It can elevate its body temperature a few degrees above the temperature of the surrounding water (very uncommon for a fish). Scientists think they do it in order to make their muscles more efficient. This allows the Mako to be one of the fastest sharks in the world, able to swim in short bursts up to 100 km/h! They do it to catch their favourite food: large game fish like tuna.

Opposite top: Drawn by bait, but wary of the photographer, a Caribbean Reef shark *(Carcharhinus perezi)* approaches cautiously. Underwater, scuba divers are as frightening to a shark as a shark is to us.

Opposite bottom: A stingray is a close relative of sharks and has all of the attributes of a shark, except for shape. It has a skeleton made of cartilage, multiple gill slits (hidden underneath the body where they can't be seen), sandpapery skin, and no swim bladder.

Reproduction

The long evolution of sharks and rays has allowed them to diversify into just about every marine habitat and develop powerful adaptations for survival. As sharks and rays are a varied group of animals, so are their reproductive mechanisms.

All sharks copulate and then fertilise internally. What happens from there depends on the species. Reproduction occurs in one of three different ways. *Oviparous* species like the Horn shark *(Heterodontus francisci)* lay large, tough eggs on the bottom, which incubate for periods up to a year. Each egg contains a large yolk sac, providing nourishment for the developing embryo. Many skates also reproduce by laying eggs.

Right: Sand Tiger sharks *(Carcharias Taurus)* can be found at certain times of the year around certain shipwrecks in North Carolina, USA. Biologists think they aggregate at the wrecks to mate. This is one of the few ways to see sharks without chumming. This shark is cruising through the wreck of the Atlas, about 40 km off the coast of North Carolina.

Opposite: After a gestation period of 6 to 9 months, a Little Skate *(Raja erinacea)* emerges from its egg case. The baby skate is only 5 centimetres long and will have to fend for itself.

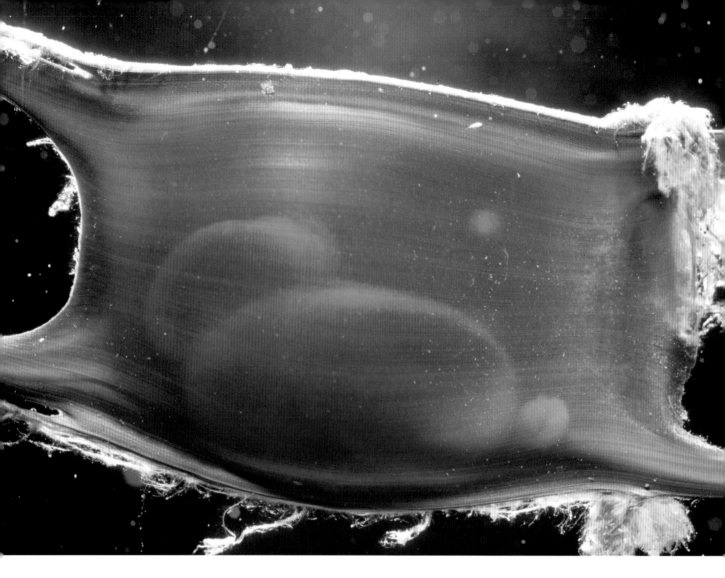

Viviparous sharks nourish their developing embryos using a placental system strikingly similar to our own. They have a uterus in which one to as many as 100 embryos develop, each nourished by an umbilical cord from the mother. When the babies are born, the umbilical cords break and the baby sharks emerge from the mother's uterus just like a mammal would be born.

Previous page: Talk about a wide mouth! A Whale shark's mouth can be 2 metres across. Swimming with a shark the size of a school bus is a huge adrenalin rush!

Above: A baby Little skate *(Raja erinacea)* develops within its egg case. Females lay the eggs on the bottom of the North Atlantic year around. Inside the egg, the large blob at the bottom is the yolk which provides nourishment to the tiny embryo. As the embryo grows, the yolk shrinks.

Opposite: Contrary to popular belief, most sharks are no danger to people. The Horn shark *(Heterodontus francisci)* lives in the coastal waters of California and feeds mostly on sea urchins and other small invertebrates. It is oviparous, meaning that it reproduces by laying eggs.

Ovoviviparous sharks are like a combination of the other two types, in which the mother produces eggs with a very thin membrane "shell" that are held internally until they hatch. Once they break the membrane, the embryonic sharks stay within the mother's uterus to develop until birth. During birth, ovoviviparous sharks have the appearance of viviparous sharks because the baby sharks emerge awake and swimming. Since the developing embryos have no placental nourishment, ovoviviparous sharks nourish the developing embryos in one of several ways. In some sharks, like the Great White *(Carcharodon carcharias)*, the embryos get their nourishment by eating unfertilised eggs supplied by the mother for that purpose. In some species, like the Sand Tiger shark *(Carcharias taurus)*, the embryonic sharks engage in prenatal intra-uterine cannibalism, where the strongest or first born of the embryos eats the other embryos or unhatched eggs to provide nourishment for themselves. Since the Sand Tiger has two uteri, each one produces only one baby shark, because the strongest one eats all its brothers and sisters! Ovoviviparous reproduction is also called *aplacental viviparity.*

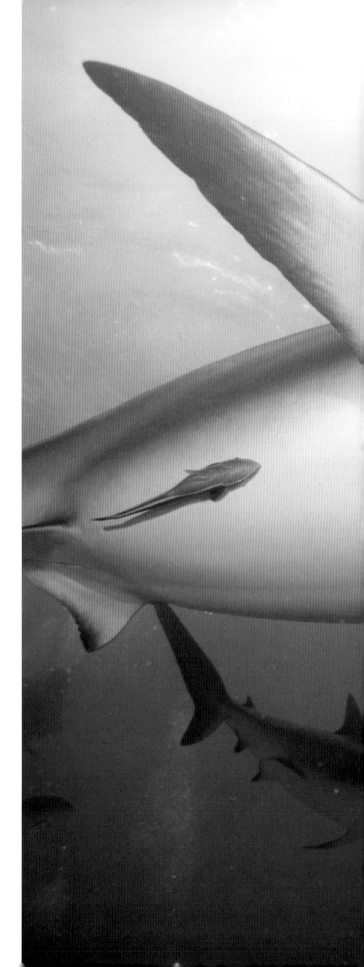

Sharks do not protect their offspring once they have been born. Baby sharks are born ready and able to survive on their own. The typical bony fish produces thousands of tiny helpless planktonic offspring at a time, most of which get eaten before they mature. Rather than attempt to overwhelm predators with a large quantity of vulnerable offspring like most fishes, sharks produce a much smaller number of more resilient juveniles. Baby sharks tend to be born considerably larger and more developed than most fishes. To accomplish this, most species of sharks have long gestation periods, some even longer than human gestation periods.

The longest known gestation period of any animal in the world is believed to be in a shark, a whopping three and a half years for the Frilled Shark *(Chlamydoselachus anguineus)*. Most do not last that long, but many last much longer than the nine month gestation period in humans. The Spiny Dogfish *(Squalus acanthias)* has a gestation period of 20-22 months.

Previous page: This female Great White *(Carcharodon carcharias)* has scars all over her body from mating. Males bite the females to hold on to them during mating. Because mating is so hard on the females, they have skin that is twice as thick as the males.

Right: The small fish attached to this Caribbean Reef shark *(Carcharhinus perezi)* behind its pectoral fin is called a remora or shark sucker. This fish actually has a suction cup on its head and it attaches itself to sharks, dolphins, whales and turtles for a free ride. It eats parasites from the shark and scraps of leftover food. They probably annoy the sharks though because sharks frequently try to shake them off.

As much as we know about the Great White shark *(Carcharodon carcharias)* we have no idea how long its gestation period is. The Whale shark *(Rhincodon typus)* might be the world's largest fish, but that doesn't make it easy to study. Biologists thought it was oviparous until 1996 when a pregnant female harpooned by fishermen was examined by a team of biologists. They found 300 embryonic sharks in her uterus! Now we know that the Whale shark is ovoviviparous, though we still don't know how long the gestation period is.

The diversity of sharks is mirrored by their complicated reproductive strategies. We should expect no less from an animal that has been swimming in the oceans for millions of years.

Above: A newborn Little Skate *(Raja erinacea)* rests beside the egg it emerged from. The eggs of skates often wash up on shore. They are often called "mermaid's purses" and people mistake them for dried up seaweed.

Right: In the 1980's heavy fishing for Sand Tiger sharks *(Carcharias Taurus)* dramatically reduced the number of these sharks in the Atlantic ocean. Virtually no Sand Tigers were seen in North Carolina for many years. Today, Sand Tigers are protected by law in the U.S., Australia and other countries, and they are making a come back.

Next page: A pregnant Sand Tiger *(Carcharias Taurus)* with a distended belly. She is likely very close to delivering her pups. Sand Tigers only produce two pups because the two largest embryos eat all their siblings while they are still in the mother's uterus! This unique method of nourishing the embryos, called intrauterine cannibalism, is rare.

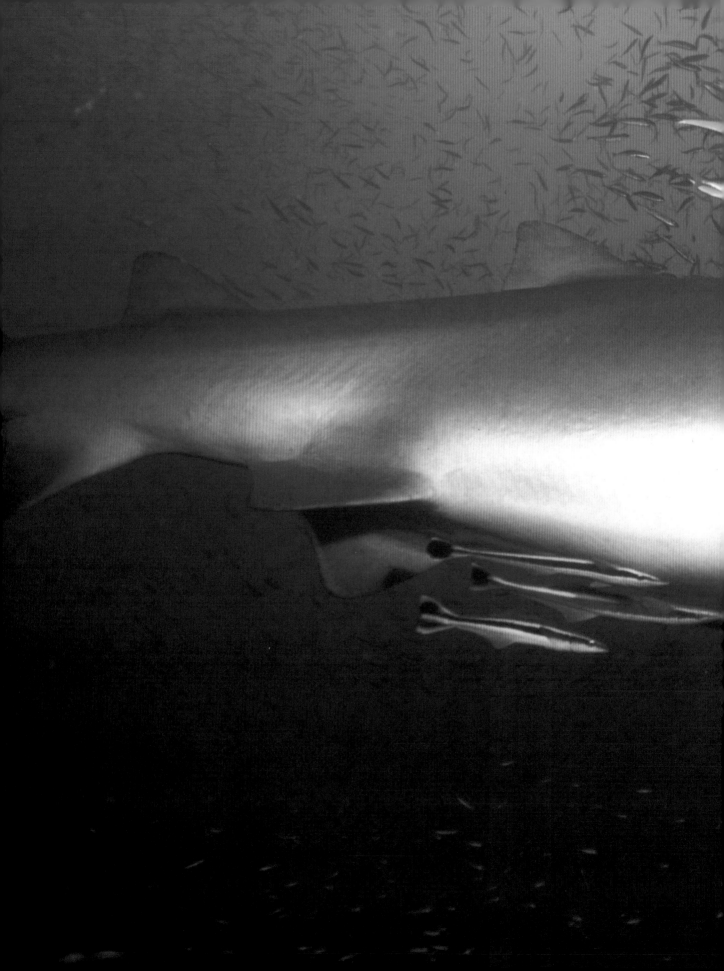

Sharks and Man

In the modern world, mankind has little fear of monsters. Very few people will ever seriously worry about being eaten by a lion or attacked by a bear. It's even less likely that any of us will ever be attacked by a shark, and yet most people are still frightened of sharks. The myth that sharks eat people has been perpetuated throughout history with startling regularity. The fact is, less than 10 fatal shark attacks occur every year in the entire world. You are much more likely to be killed in a car, by a dog, or even by lightning than you are to be attacked by a shark.

Certainly sharks can eat people, but the simple fact is that they almost never do. Between the years of 1990 and 1996, there were an average of 50 attacks of sharks on people per year throughout the entire world, and less than 15% of these were fatal (on average, less than 8 per year). Statistically, sharks are no more dangerous to people than any other large predator, like a tiger or a lion. We crown the lion "King of the Jungle" and yet label the shark a "man-eating killer."

Above: A 5.5 metre, 1,350 kg female Great White *(Carcharodon carcharias)* accidentally caught in a fisherman's net in Massachusetts, USA. Because the Great White shark has been hunted heavily in the past and has a very slow rate of reproduction, the population of these apex predators has been shrinking around the world.

Right: In the waters off Hawaii, an Oceanic White Tip shark *(Carcharhinus longimanus)* cruises in search of a meal. In these waters, Oceanic White Tips are frequently seen following pods of pilot whales. Nobody is certain why the sharks associate with the whales. They don't feed on them. In 2004 while filming them for a television program, I witnessed Oceanic White Tips feeding on the faeces of the whales, which may provide a clue why they follow the whales!

It hardly seems fair, especially when dogs, snakes, crocodiles, hippopotamuses, elephants and even bees kill many more people every year than sharks.

On the rare occasion when a person is attacked by a shark, there are three general reasons why it might happen. The first one makes the most sense, but is likely the least common – food. Sometimes large aggressive sharks like Tiger sharks or Great White sharks attack people as a source of food. But, usually by accident – the shark thinking the person was something else. In areas off California, Great White shark attacks on people almost always involve swimmers and surfers, but very rarely divers. Because the sharks frequently feed on sea lions that swim at the surface, sharks probably think the swimmers and surfers are sea lions. This behaviour can hardly be called aggressive – the shark just wanted something to eat and made an error. In Hawaii, Tiger sharks feed on sea turtles and can sometimes make a similar mistake when attacking people paddling surf boards.

Right: A Blue shark *(Prionace glauca)* has been tagged. If this shark is ever caught, with luck the tag will be returned to the U.S. National Marine Fisheries Service so they can learn where this shark went after it was tagged in New England.

Sharks also attack people when they are defending themselves (or *think* they are defending themselves). These "provoked attacks" happen when divers harass them, when sharks are caught on a hook and reeled into a boat, or when they are put into any situation where the instinct for survival takes over. We hear on the news about a shark attack where someone was injured and everyone jumps to the conclusion that some "bad" shark attacked without reason. Reports may ignore that the shark was caught on a hook and line, and trying to escape. If you were caught on a hook, wouldn't you bite someone to get away?

Opposite: It's not so hard to see why a shark might mistake a person on a surfboard for a seal or a turtle!

Below: A diver takes a tissue sample from a large Whale shark *(Rhincodon typus)* in the Galapagos for a study on genetics.

Overleaf: This Blue shark *(Prionace glauca)* has been permanently disfigured by a fisherman. When sharks are caught on a hook, sometimes fishermen slash the mouth of the shark to get rid of it. Often the shark dies, but sometimes the shark can survive with its wounds. Its better than becoming shark fin soup!

Very rarely sharks attack people for no particular reason, called an unprovoked attack. I know two different people that were badly bitten by Gray Reef sharks on separate occasions. In one case, the photographer took a picture of the shark as it swam past and the shark reacted by turning and biting him. What he had not known at the time was that the shark felt threatened because the diver had entered its "turf." It was putting on an antagonistic display (called threat posturing) swimming in jerky movements with its pectoral fins down and its back hunched up. Some species of sharks do this when they are agitated. Other sharks can read that body language, but until recently we humans didn't know about it.

We now know that when a Gray Reef shark starts threat posturing, you need to get as far away from that shark as fast as possible. At the time the photographer took his picture, nobody knew about threat posturing in sharks. When he snapped the picture, the flash probably frightened the agitated shark and, in defence it bit him. This attack seemed unprovoked, but in retrospect, the signs were there, though unrecognised. It is likely that many apparently unprovoked attacks by sharks really were provoked in some way known only to the shark.

Right: Charlie Donilon in New England runs a dive boat catering to diving with Blue sharks. Here he chops up small fish to attract sharks to his boat. This is called chumming.

Another fact to remember is that only a few species of sharks are dangerous (like Great Whites, Tiger sharks and Bull sharks to name a few). The vast majority present no threat to people at all either because of their diminutive size, or their shy personality. Yes, some sharks occasionally attack people, and there is need for care in waters containing sharks, but attacks are incredibly rare and there is no reason to be irrationally fearful about them.

Ironically, sharks may in fact save many human lives. Research on sharks is paving the way to new discoveries in science that will help develop new medicines and treatments for human diseases.

Above: In the Neptune Islands of South Australia, we begin the chumming process to lure Great White sharks to the boat. A mixture of chicken blood, tuna oil and fish blood creates a scent trail, while tuna chucks tied with twine act as lures that the sharks can't resist.

Right: A Blue shark *(Prionace glauca)* has grabbed a bait. This shot shows how the shark closes its nictitating membranes to protect its eyes. This renders the shark blind while it's fighting with prey.

Above: Lowering the shark cage
into the water is a precaution
when diving with Blue sharks.

Left: Most of the time, the cage
is not necessary. Blue sharks are
generally quite docile.

For example, the highly evolved and extremely sensitive nervous systems of sharks make excellent subjects for the study of nerves. Shark eyes, similar to those of humans, have lenses that readily form cataracts upon exposure to ultraviolet light in a way similar to human eyes. The study of cataracts in sharks may provide new ways of preventing and treating the condition in people.

Below: The chum trail has been started. Now we wait for sharks!

Right: At last, a Great White *(Carcharodon carcharias)* takes the bait. There is nothing like the sight of a White shark going for a bait!

Shark rectal glands, which maintain the shark's osmotic (salt) balance, have been used in the study of cystic fibrosis, a deadly human genetic disease. The shark heart produces potent hormones that regulate its kidneys. In humans, drugs created from derivatives of these hormones control blood pressure, relieve angina symptoms, and reduce the risk of heart attacks by acting as calcium blockers.

It has long been known that sharks have very low incidence of cancers in their tissues. This has lead to the widespread proliferation of a variety of bogus "health products" made from the cartilage of sharks, reputed to prevent or cure cancer in humans. It has no such effect and serves only to further destroy shark populations.

Overleaf: The Caribbean Reef shark (Carcharhinus perezi) gets its name because it lives around coral reefs where it finds abundant tropical fish and squid to eat. It does not think of a human as food. The only way this shark might attack a person would be when threatened.

The shark immune systems seem designed to inhibit cancers. For a tumour to develop, it needs nutrients that it can only get from a blood supply. Shark tissues contain special enzymes that inhibit vascularisation (the formation of blood vesicles), a crucial step in the formation of tumours. Without a supply of nutrients from the blood, tumours simply cannot grow. The hope of finding new drugs for treating cancer has prompted renewed research into the anti-tumour properties of sharks.

Recent research has shown that shark stomachs produce a new kind of powerful antibiotic steroids (called squalamines) that are now being developed to treat human diseases. Who knows what incredible discoveries await scientists exploring the mysteries of such highly evolved and adapted animals as sharks? Though we may fear sharks, they may prove themselves extremely beneficial to people. For that, we owe them a little respect. Instead, we are wiping them out.

All over the world, shark populations are down, as a result of tremendous overfishing. Sharks reproduce few offspring and they do so very slowly, taking quite a few years to reach maturity. In fact, very few cultures eat shark meat since the high amount of urea in their flesh means they do not taste very flavoursome. Sharks are most often caught in nets by accident or for their fins.

Previous page: This Oceanic White Tip shark *(Carcharhinus longimanus)* has a companion, called a pilot fish. Pilot fish got their name because people used to think the shark was following the fish. Now we know that the fish is really just a moocher looking for some free food from the shark's messy eating habits and if the fish isn't careful, it might end up as lunch!

Opposite: Silky sharks *(Carcharhinus falciformis)* are found in the same places where big game fish live—the open ocean. Sport fishermen fishing for Marlin and other big game fishes sometimes catch sharks. When they catch Silky sharks, they usually just cut the line and throw the shark back rather than attempt to get the hook out of the shark's mouth.

Above: A Great White shark *(Carcharodon carcharias)* circles the cage! Few things in life are as exciting as that!

Right: Shark diving is not all fun and games. Sometimes we spend hours in the cage waiting for a Great White shark to make a close pass for pictures.

Most sharks can't survive for long when caught in a net. Because a lot of species can't ventilate their gills unless they are swimming, they quickly suffocate. So when the fisherman pulls in his nets, he has dead sharks for which there is little to no market. He throws them back dead, a huge and heartbreaking waste.

One of the other driving forces in the overfishing of sharks is the demand for shark fins in Asian markets. Perhaps the most cruel and destructive method of fishing for sharks is the process of *shark finning*. Sharks are caught and dragged aboard a boat where the fins are cut off while the shark is still alive, then, the poor creature is thrown back into the ocean to die. Without fins it cannot swim or stay off the bottom. The shark sinks to the bottom and slowly dies, either by suffocation or starvation. Never mind the inherent cruelty of this practice, it is also wasteful.

Why such a demand for shark fins? In Asia, shark fin soup is a delicacy. Contrary to popular belief, shark fin soup is *not* considered an aphrodisiac. In fact, shark fin soup to Asians is more like caviar to westerners – a food served by the wealthy designed to exhibit success or class. But unlike caviar, which at least has flavour of its own, shark fins have no taste. The soup actually gets all its flavour from chicken. The soup is prepared from normal chicken broth, with the shark fins added for texture.

Above: A Blue shark *(Prionace glauca)* has grabbed a piece of bait. The sharp teeth are evident!

Opposite top: When the sharks are acting a little aggressive, some divers stay half in the cage in case they need to make a quick retreat.

Bottom right: Shark dives are proven money-makers for dive operators as more and more people want to see sharks in their natural habitat. The sharks on some islands in the Caribbean are worth millions of dollars per year in tourist income – far more than their value in a fishing boat.

The fins themselves, once removed from the shark, are dried. When they reach the restaurant to be prepared, they are boiled for hours, until they disintegrate. The thin strips of cartilage that give the fin stiffness separate from each other and take on the consistency and appearance of cooked spaghetti. Once the chicken broth is ready, the shark fin cartilage is added at the last minute like noodles and then the soup is served.

Historically, shark fins were rare and thus expensive. The long preparation time combined with cost made shark fin soup exclusive, so it became a status symbol to be served at special occasions. With the increase in the availability of shark fins and a marked reduction in price, shark fin soup has become more accessible to the general public and is no longer difficult to get or expensive, yet the soup retains its exclusive tag. Now anyone can afford to be "high class" and order shark fin soup at their favourite restaurant. There is a huge market for shark fins that fishermen are eager to fill.

Previous page: Although it gets is name from the place where it was first sighted, the Galapagos shark *(Carcharhinus galapagensis)* lives throughout a wide range of the Pacific Ocean. This graceful and sleek shark was photographed at Midway Atoll, north of Hawaii.

Left: Contrary to popular belief, it's rare to see more than one shark at a time. Most sharks are solitary animals, preferring to hunt by themselves. This pair of Caribbean Reef sharks have been attracted to the same area using bait.

Below: Dried shark fins in a shop in Malaysia are prepared for the shark fin soup trade. The demand for this Asian delicacy is devastating shark populations worldwide.

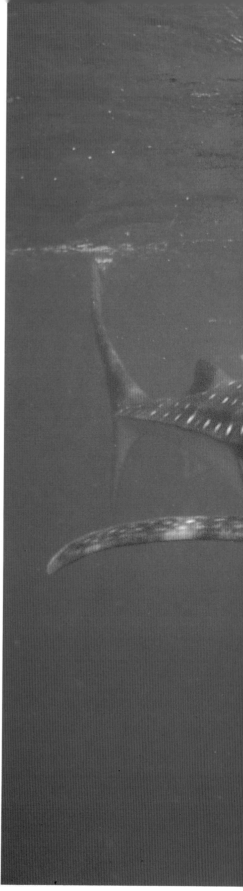

In recent years, public outcry has started to put a little bit of pressure on shark fishing industries and supporters of it. As a result several Asian airlines have stopped serving shark fin soup and countries such as the United States have finally outlawed shark finning (the legislation was passed in late 2000). With continued education and effort, it may be possible to eliminate this wasteful and destructive practice but until there is no demand for shark fin soup it will sadly continue.

Above: A researcher with a satellite tag on a spear gun. He is looking for a Whale shark to tag at Darwin Island, Galapagos. The skin of a Whale shark is so thick (up to 17 cm) and tough that it takes a powerful spear gun to implant the tag!

Right: Off Western Australia, a Whale shark cruises the open ocean with its mouth open, feeding on tiny planktonic animals. The small fish near its mouth is not food. It's using the shark as a big bodyguard, staying only inches from the shark to avoid being eaten by other predators.

Overleaf: Which is more dangerous? Believe it or not, the Lion's Mane Jelly *(Cyanea capillata)* is far more likely to be a threat to a diver than the Blue shark.

Fortunately, sharks have their supporters, and they often come from what might be considered an unusual group of people: divers. Perhaps no other group of people are so interested in seeing sharks maintain healthy populations. Shark diving eco-tourism is now one of the strongest arguments for maintaining healthy shark populations: they are worth more alive than dead. One Bahamian shark diving operation has estimated that their local population of a dozen reef sharks is worth more than a million dollars a year in the tourism revenue that they generate. Yet those same few sharks would be worth a few hundred dollars to a fisherman in shark fins. Sometimes, it's only the power of money that makes a compelling argument.

Ultimately, we as caretakers of the planet must realise that sharks are important to the ecosystem, and their millions of years of evolution may hold the secrets to curing human diseases. For these reasons alone, it is not just our responsibility to protect them, but a smart thing to do as well. The fact is, we might end up needing sharks a lot more than they need us.

Left: After implanting a satellite tag on a Whale shark
(*Rhincodon typus*), a researcher is removing the pole
spear. The tag will record data about the shark for
6 months and then pop off, float to the surface and
transmit its data to a satellite. The data will reveal all
kinds of things about the mysterious Whale shark such
as where it goes and how deep it dives.

Above: While feeding, the gill slits of this Basking shark
(*Cetorhinus maximus*) are open so wide that you can see
the gills themselves. A shark this big needs huge gills,
but not so much for their ability to extract oxygen from
the water as for their ability to strain plankton.

Right: The Basking shark got its name because mariners
saw them at the surface and thought they were sunning
themselves, or basking. Later it was discovered that
they come to the surface when it's calm to feed on
clouds of plankton just under the surface. Often, they
are feeding so close to the surface that the dorsal fin
sticks up above the water.

Overleaf: Sharks will closely approach divers that feed
them, but they seem quite capable of differentiating
between the diver and the food. Even at such close
range as this, divers are rarely bitten by sharks.